Guest Book

Celebrating

Date

Place

Guest Name

Top ParentingTip

Special Message to Baby

Guest Name

Top ParentingTip

Special Message to Baby

Guest Name

_____

_____

Top Parenting Tip

_____

_____

_____

_____

_____

Special Message to Baby

_____

_____

_____

_____

Guest Name

_____

_____

Top Parenting Tip

_____

_____

_____

_____

_____

Special Message to Baby

_____

_____

_____

_____

Guest Name

_____

_____

Top Parenting Tip

_____

_____

_____

_____

Special Message to Baby

_____

_____

_____

_____

Guest Name

_____

_____

Top Parenting Tip

_____

_____

_____

_____

Special Message to Baby

_____

_____

_____

_____

Guest Name

_____

_____

Top Parenting Tip

_____

_____

_____

_____

_____

Special Message to Baby

_____

_____

_____

_____

Guest Name

_____

_____

Top Parenting Tip

_____

_____

_____

_____

_____

Special Message to Baby

_____

_____

_____

_____

Guest Name

_____

Top Parenting Tip

_____
_____
_____
_____

Special Message to Baby

_____
_____
_____
_____

Guest Name

_____

Top Parenting Tip

_____
_____
_____
_____

Special Message to Baby

_____
_____
_____
_____

Guest Name

_____

_____

Top Parenting Tip

_____

_____

_____

_____

_____

Special Message to Baby

_____

_____

_____

_____

Guest Name

_____

_____

Top Parenting Tip

_____

_____

_____

_____

_____

Special Message to Baby

_____

_____

_____

_____

Guest Name

Top Parenting Tip

_____

_____

_____

_____

Special Message to Baby

_____

_____

_____

_____

Guest Name

Top Parenting Tip

_____

_____

_____

_____

Special Message to Baby

_____

_____

_____

_____

Guest Name

Top Parenting Tip

Special Message to Baby

Guest Name

Top Parenting Tip

Special Message to Baby

Guest Name

Top Parenting Tip

Special Message to Baby

Guest Name

Top Parenting Tip

Special Message to Baby

Guest Name

_____

_____

Top Parenting Tip

_____

_____

_____

_____

_____

Special Message to Baby

_____

_____

_____

_____

_____

Guest Name

_____

_____

Top Parenting Tip

_____

_____

_____

_____

_____

Special Message to Baby

_____

_____

_____

_____

_____

Guest Name

_____

Top Parenting Tip

_____

_____

_____

_____

Special Message to Baby

_____

_____

_____

_____

Guest Name

_____

Top Parenting Tip

_____

_____

_____

_____

Special Message to Baby

_____

_____

_____

_____

Guest Name

_____

Top ParentingTip

_____
_____
_____
_____
_____

Special Message to Baby

_____
_____
_____
_____

Guest Name

_____

Top ParentingTip

_____
_____
_____
_____
_____

Special Message to Baby

_____
_____
_____
_____

Guest Name

Top ParentingTip

Special Message to Baby

Guest Name

Top ParentingTip

Special Message to Baby

Guest Name

_____

_____

Top Parenting Tip

_____

_____

_____

_____

_____

_____

Special Message to Baby

_____

_____

_____

_____

_____

Guest Name

_____

_____

Top Parenting Tip

_____

_____

_____

_____

_____

_____

Special Message to Baby

_____

_____

_____

_____

_____

Guest Name

_____

_____

Top Parenting Tip

_____

_____

_____

_____

_____

Special Message to Baby

_____

_____

_____

_____

Guest Name

_____

_____

Top Parenting Tip

_____

_____

_____

_____

_____

Special Message to Baby

_____

_____

_____

_____

Guest Name

Top Parenting Tip

Special Message to Baby

Guest Name

Top Parenting Tip

Special Message to Baby

Guest Name

Top Parenting Tip

Special Message to Baby

Guest Name

Top Parenting Tip

Special Message to Baby

Guest Name

_____

_____

Top Parenting Tip

_____

_____

_____

_____

_____

Special Message to Baby

_____

_____

_____

_____

Guest Name

_____

_____

Top Parenting Tip

_____

_____

_____

_____

_____

Special Message to Baby

_____

_____

_____

_____

Guest Name

_____

Top Parenting Tip

_____

_____

_____

_____

_____

Special Message to Baby

_____

_____

_____

_____

Guest Name

_____

Top Parenting Tip

_____

_____

_____

_____

_____

Special Message to Baby

_____

_____

_____

_____

Guest Name

_____

_____

Top Parenting Tip

_____

_____

_____

_____

_____

Special Message to Baby

_____

_____

_____

_____

_____

Guest Name

_____

_____

Top Parenting Tip

_____

_____

_____

_____

_____

Special Message to Baby

_____

_____

_____

_____

_____

Guest Name

_____

_____

Top Parenting Tip

_____

_____

_____

_____

_____

Special Message to Baby

_____

_____

_____

_____

Guest Name

_____

_____

Top Parenting Tip

_____

_____

_____

_____

_____

Special Message to Baby

_____

_____

_____

_____

Guest Name

_____

_____

Top Parenting Tip

_____

_____

_____

_____

_____

Special Message to Baby

_____

_____

_____

_____

Guest Name

_____

_____

Top Parenting Tip

_____

_____

_____

_____

_____

Special Message to Baby

_____

_____

_____

_____

Guest Name

_____

_____

Top Parenting Tip

_____

_____

_____

_____

_____

Special Message to Baby

_____

_____

_____

_____

_____

Guest Name

_____

_____

Top Parenting Tip

_____

_____

_____

_____

_____

Special Message to Baby

_____

_____

_____

_____

_____

Guest Name

_____

_____

Top Parenting Tip

_____

_____

_____

_____

_____

Special Message to Baby

_____

_____

_____

_____

_____

Guest Name

_____

_____

Top Parenting Tip

_____

_____

_____

_____

_____

Special Message to Baby

_____

_____

_____

_____

_____

Guest Name

Guest Name

Top Parenting Tip

Top Parenting Tip

Special Message to Baby

Special Message to Baby

Guest Name

_____

_____

Top Parenting Tip

_____

_____

_____

_____

_____

Special Message to Baby

_____

_____

_____

_____

_____

Guest Name

_____

_____

Top Parenting Tip

_____

_____

_____

_____

_____

Special Message to Baby

_____

_____

_____

_____

_____

Guest Name

_____

Top Parenting Tip

_____
_____
_____
_____

Special Message to Baby

_____
_____
_____

Guest Name

_____

Top Parenting Tip

_____
_____
_____
_____

Special Message to Baby

_____
_____
_____

Guest Name

_____

_____

Top Parenting Tip

_____

_____

_____

_____

_____

_____

Special Message to Baby

_____

_____

_____

_____

_____

Guest Name

_____

_____

Top Parenting Tip

_____

_____

_____

_____

_____

_____

Special Message to Baby

_____

_____

_____

_____

_____

Guest Name

_____

_____

Top Parenting Tip

_____

_____

_____

_____

_____

Special Message to Baby

_____

_____

_____

_____

_____

Guest Name

_____

_____

Top Parenting Tip

_____

_____

_____

_____

_____

Special Message to Baby

_____

_____

_____

_____

_____

Guest Name

_____

_____

Top Parenting Tip

_____

_____

_____

_____

_____

Special Message to Baby

_____

_____

_____

_____

Guest Name

_____

_____

Top Parenting Tip

_____

_____

_____

_____

_____

Special Message to Baby

_____

_____

_____

_____

Guest Name

Top Parenting Tip

Special Message to Baby

Guest Name

Top Parenting Tip

Special Message to Baby

Guest Name

_____

_____

Top Parenting Tip

_____

_____

_____

_____

_____

_____

Special Message to Baby

_____

_____

_____

_____

_____

Guest Name

_____

_____

Top Parenting Tip

_____

_____

_____

_____

_____

_____

Special Message to Baby

_____

_____

_____

_____

_____

Guest Name

_____

Top Parenting Tip

_____

_____

_____

_____

Special Message to Baby

_____

_____

_____

_____

Guest Name

_____

Top Parenting Tip

_____

_____

_____

_____

Special Message to Baby

_____

_____

_____

_____

Guest Name

_____

_____

Top Parenting Tip

_____

_____

_____

_____

_____

Special Message to Baby

_____

_____

_____

_____

_____

Guest Name

_____

_____

Top Parenting Tip

_____

_____

_____

_____

_____

Special Message to Baby

_____

_____

_____

_____

_____

Guest Name

Top Parenting Tip

Special Message to Baby

Guest Name

Top Parenting Tip

Special Message to Baby

Guest Name

_____

_____

Top Parenting Tip

_____

_____

_____

_____

_____

Special Message to Baby

_____

_____

_____

_____

_____

Guest Name

_____

_____

Top Parenting Tip

_____

_____

_____

_____

_____

Special Message to Baby

_____

_____

_____

_____

_____

Guest Name

Top Parenting Tip

Special Message to Baby

Guest Name

Top Parenting Tip

Special Message to Baby

Guest Name

_____

_____

Top Parenting Tip

_____

_____

_____

_____

_____

Special Message to Baby

_____

_____

_____

_____

Guest Name

_____

_____

Top Parenting Tip

_____

_____

_____

_____

_____

Special Message to Baby

_____

_____

_____

_____

Guest Name

_____

_____

Top Parenting Tip

_____

_____

_____

_____

_____

Special Message to Baby

_____

_____

_____

_____

Guest Name

_____

_____

Top Parenting Tip

_____

_____

_____

_____

_____

Special Message to Baby

_____

_____

_____

_____

Guest Name

_____

_____

Top Parenting Tip

_____

_____

_____

_____

_____

Special Message to Baby

_____

_____

_____

_____

_____

Guest Name

_____

_____

Top Parenting Tip

_____

_____

_____

_____

_____

Special Message to Baby

_____

_____

_____

_____

_____

Guest Name

_____

_____

Top Parenting Tip

_____

_____

_____

_____

_____

Special Message to Baby

_____

_____

_____

_____

_____

Guest Name

_____

_____

Top Parenting Tip

_____

_____

_____

_____

_____

Special Message to Baby

_____

_____

_____

_____

_____

Guest Name

_____

_____

Top ParentingTip

_____

_____

_____

_____

_____

Special Message to Baby

_____

_____

_____

_____

Guest Name

_____

_____

Top ParentingTip

_____

_____

_____

_____

_____

Special Message to Baby

_____

_____

_____

_____

Guest Name

_____

Top Parenting Tip

_____

_____

_____

_____

_____

Special Message to Baby

_____

_____

_____

_____

Guest Name

_____

Top Parenting Tip

_____

_____

_____

_____

_____

Special Message to Baby

_____

_____

_____

_____

Guest Name

_____

_____

Top Parenting Tip

_____

_____

_____

_____

_____

Special Message to Baby

_____

_____

_____

_____

_____

Guest Name

_____

_____

Top Parenting Tip

_____

_____

_____

_____

_____

Special Message to Baby

_____

_____

_____

_____

_____

Guest Name

_____

Top Parenting Tip

_____

_____

_____

_____

Special Message to Baby

_____

_____

_____

Guest Name

_____

Top Parenting Tip

_____

_____

_____

_____

Special Message to Baby

_____

_____

_____

Guest Name

_____

_____

Top Parenting Tip

_____

_____

_____

_____

_____

_____

Special Message to Baby

_____

_____

_____

_____

_____

Guest Name

_____

_____

Top Parenting Tip

_____

_____

_____

_____

_____

_____

Special Message to Baby

_____

_____

_____

_____

_____

Guest Name

Top Parenting Tip

Special Message to Baby

Guest Name

Top Parenting Tip

Special Message to Baby

Guest Name

_____

Top Parenting Tip

_____

_____

_____

_____

_____

Special Message to Baby

_____

_____

_____

_____

Guest Name

_____

Top Parenting Tip

_____

_____

_____

_____

_____

Special Message to Baby

_____

_____

_____

_____

Guest Name

_____

_____

Top Parenting Tip

_____

_____

_____

_____

_____

Special Message to Baby

_____

_____

_____

_____

Guest Name

_____

_____

Top Parenting Tip

_____

_____

_____

_____

_____

Special Message to Baby

_____

_____

_____

_____

Guest Name

_____

Top ParentingTip

_____

_____

_____

_____

_____

Special Message to Baby

_____

_____

_____

_____

Guest Name

_____

Top ParentingTip

_____

_____

_____

_____

_____

Special Message to Baby

_____

_____

_____

_____

Guest Name

_____

Top Parenting Tip

_____

_____

_____

_____

_____

Special Message to Baby

_____

_____

_____

_____

Guest Name

_____

Top Parenting Tip

_____

_____

_____

_____

_____

Special Message to Baby

_____

_____

_____

_____

Guest Name

_____

_____

Top Parenting Tip

_____

_____

_____

_____

_____

Special Message to Baby

_____

_____

_____

_____

Guest Name

_____

_____

Top Parenting Tip

_____

_____

_____

_____

_____

Special Message to Baby

_____

_____

_____

_____

Guest Name

_____

Top Parenting Tip

_____
_____
_____
_____
_____

Special Message to Baby

_____
_____
_____
_____

Guest Name

_____

Top Parenting Tip

_____
_____
_____
_____
_____

Special Message to Baby

_____
_____
_____
_____

Guest Name

_____

_____

Top Parenting Tip

_____

_____

_____

_____

_____

_____

Special Message to Baby

_____

_____

_____

_____

_____

Guest Name

_____

_____

Top Parenting Tip

_____

_____

_____

_____

_____

_____

Special Message to Baby

_____

_____

_____

_____

_____

Guest Name

Top Parenting Tip

Special Message to Baby

Guest Name

Top Parenting Tip

Special Message to Baby

Guest Name

_____

_____

Top ParentingTip

_____

_____

_____

_____

_____

_____

Special Message to Baby

_____

_____

_____

_____

_____

Guest Name

_____

_____

Top ParentingTip

_____

_____

_____

_____

_____

_____

Special Message to Baby

_____

_____

_____

_____

_____

Guest Name

_____

Top Parenting Tip

_____

_____

_____

_____

_____

Special Message to Baby

_____

_____

_____

_____

Guest Name

_____

Top Parenting Tip

_____

_____

_____

_____

_____

Special Message to Baby

_____

_____

_____

_____

Guest Name

_____

_____

Top Parenting Tip

_____

_____

_____

_____

_____

Special Message to Baby

_____

_____

_____

_____

_____

Guest Name

_____

_____

Top Parenting Tip

_____

_____

_____

_____

_____

Special Message to Baby

_____

_____

_____

_____

_____

Guest Name

_____

_____

Top Parenting Tip

_____

_____

_____

_____

_____

Special Message to Baby

_____

_____

_____

_____

Guest Name

_____

_____

Top Parenting Tip

_____

_____

_____

_____

_____

Special Message to Baby

_____

_____

_____

_____

Guest Name

_____

_____

Top Parenting Tip

_____

_____

_____

_____

_____

Special Message to Baby

_____

_____

_____

_____

Guest Name

_____

_____

Top Parenting Tip

_____

_____

_____

_____

_____

Special Message to Baby

_____

_____

_____

_____

Guest Name

_____

Top ParentingTip

_____

_____

_____

_____

_____

Special Message to Baby

_____

_____

_____

_____

Guest Name

_____

Top ParentingTip

_____

_____

_____

_____

_____

Special Message to Baby

_____

_____

_____

_____

Guest Name

_____

Top Parenting Tip

_____
_____
_____
_____

Special Message to Baby

_____
_____
_____
_____

Guest Name

_____

Top Parenting Tip

_____
_____
_____
_____

Special Message to Baby

_____
_____
_____
_____

Guest Name

_____

_____

Top Parenting Tip

_____

_____

_____

_____

_____

Special Message to Baby

_____

_____

_____

_____

Guest Name

_____

_____

Top Parenting Tip

_____

_____

_____

_____

_____

Special Message to Baby

_____

_____

_____

_____

Guest Name

_____

Top Parenting Tip

_____

_____

_____

_____

Special Message to Baby

_____

_____

_____

_____

Guest Name

_____

Top Parenting Tip

_____

_____

_____

_____

Special Message to Baby

_____

_____

_____

_____

Guest Name

_____

Top Parenting Tip

_____

_____

_____

_____

_____

Special Message to Baby

_____

_____

_____

_____

Guest Name

_____

Top Parenting Tip

_____

_____

_____

_____

_____

Special Message to Baby

_____

_____

_____

_____

Guest Name

Top Parenting Tip

Special Message to Baby

Guest Name

Top Parenting Tip

Special Message to Baby

Guest Name

_____

Top ParentingTip

_____

_____

_____

_____

_____

Special Message to Baby

_____

_____

_____

_____

Guest Name

_____

Top ParentingTip

_____

_____

_____

_____

_____

Special Message to Baby

_____

_____

_____

_____

Guest Name

Top Parenting Tip

Special Message to Baby

Guest Name

Top Parenting Tip

Special Message to Baby

Guest Name

_____

Top Parenting Tip

_____

_____

_____

_____

_____

Special Message to Baby

_____

_____

_____

_____

Guest Name

_____

Top Parenting Tip

_____

_____

_____

_____

_____

Special Message to Baby

_____

_____

_____

_____

Guest Name

_____

_____

Top Parenting Tip

_____

_____

_____

_____

_____

_____

Special Message to Baby

_____

_____

_____

_____

_____

Guest Name

_____

_____

Top Parenting Tip

_____

_____

_____

_____

_____

_____

Special Message to Baby

_____

_____

_____

_____

_____

Guest Name

_____

_____

Top Parenting Tip

_____

_____

_____

_____

_____

Special Message to Baby

_____

_____

_____

_____

Guest Name

_____

_____

Top Parenting Tip

_____

_____

_____

_____

_____

Special Message to Baby

_____

_____

_____

_____

Guest Name

_____

_____

Top Parenting Tip

_____

_____

_____

_____

_____

Special Message to Baby

_____

_____

_____

_____

_____

Guest Name

_____

_____

Top Parenting Tip

_____

_____

_____

_____

_____

Special Message to Baby

_____

_____

_____

_____

_____

Guest Name

_____

_____

Top Parenting Tip

_____

_____

_____

_____

_____

Special Message to Baby

_____

_____

_____

_____

Guest Name

_____

_____

Top Parenting Tip

_____

_____

_____

_____

_____

Special Message to Baby

_____

_____

_____

_____

Guest Name

_____

Top Parenting Tip

_____

_____

_____

_____

_____

Special Message to Baby

_____

_____

_____

_____

_____

Guest Name

_____

Top Parenting Tip

_____

_____

_____

_____

_____

Special Message to Baby

_____

_____

_____

_____

_____

Guest Name

_____

Top Parenting Tip

_____

_____

_____

_____

Special Message to Baby

_____

_____

_____

Guest Name

_____

Top Parenting Tip

_____

_____

_____

_____

Special Message to Baby

_____

_____

_____

Guest Name

_____

_____

Top Parenting Tip

_____

_____

_____

_____

_____

Special Message to Baby

_____

_____

_____

_____

Guest Name

_____

_____

Top Parenting Tip

_____

_____

_____

_____

_____

Special Message to Baby

_____

_____

_____

_____

Gift Giver

Gift Description

_____   _____

_____   _____

_____   _____

_____   _____

_____   _____

_____   _____

_____   _____

_____   _____

_____   _____

_____   _____

_____   _____

_____   _____

_____   _____

_____   _____

_____   _____

Gift Giver

Gift Description

_____
_____
_____
_____
_____
_____
_____
_____
_____
_____
_____
_____
_____
_____

Gift Giver

Gift Description

_____

_____

_____

_____

_____

_____

_____

_____

_____

_____

_____

_____

_____

_____

_____

Gift Giver

Gift Description

_____

_____

_____

_____

_____

_____

_____

_____

_____

_____

_____

_____

_____

_____

_____

_____

_____

_____

_____

_____

_____

_____

_____

_____

_____

_____

_____

_____

_____

_____

Gift Giver

_____

_____

_____

_____

_____

_____

_____

_____

_____

_____

_____

_____

_____

_____

Gift Description

_____

_____

_____

_____

_____

_____

_____

_____

_____

_____

_____

_____

_____

_____

Gift Giver

Gift Description

_____

_____

_____

_____

_____

_____

_____

_____

_____

_____

_____

_____

_____

_____

_____

_____

_____

_____

_____

_____

_____

_____

_____

_____

_____

_____

_____

_____

Gift Giver

_____

_____

_____

_____

_____

_____

_____

_____

_____

_____

_____

_____

_____

_____

Gift Description

_____

_____

_____

_____

_____

_____

_____

_____

_____

_____

_____

_____

_____

_____

Gift Giver

Gift Description

_____

_____

_____

_____

_____

_____

_____

_____

_____

_____

_____

_____

_____

_____

_____

Gift Giver

Gift Description

_____   _____

_____   _____

_____   _____

_____   _____

_____   _____

_____   _____

_____   _____

_____   _____

_____   _____

_____   _____

_____   _____

_____   _____

_____   _____

_____   _____

_____   _____

Gift Giver

Gift Description

_____

_____

_____

_____

_____

_____

_____

_____

_____

_____

_____

_____

_____

_____

_____

Picture Memories

Picture Memories

Picture Memories

Picture Memories

Picture Memories

Picture Memories

Picture Memories

Picture Memories

Picture Memories

Picture Memories

Picture Memories

Picture Memories

Picture Memories

Picture Memories

Picture Memories

Picture Memories

Picture Memories

Picture Memories

Picture Memories

Picture Memories

Picture Memories

Picture Memories

Picture Memories

Picture Memories

Picture Memories

Picture Memories

Picture Memories

Picture Memories

Picture Memories

Picture Memories

Made in the USA
Monee, IL
11 February 2020